THE POWER OF COMMITMENT

Allan Macintyre Clark

THE POWER OF COMMITMENT

Vanguard Press

VANGUARD PAPERBACK

A CIP catalogue record for this title is available from the British Library.

ISBN 978-1-784655-37-2

Vanguard Press is an imprint of Pegasus Elliot MacKenzie Publishers Ltd.
www.pegasuspublishers.com

First Published in 2019

Vanguard Press
Sheraton House Castle Park
Cambridge England

Printed & Bound in Great Britain

My book of poetry, not for the fainthearted.
Weather the storm, it will hopefully be inspiring.

What follows is my pursuit in life to find true love and to be accepted as a gay man. It is brutal at times, angry at others, reflective, saddening, frustrating, enlightening, damning, uplifting, hopeful, intolerant and perhaps bitter. I only hope that it will be relatable, not just with those who have suffered the indignation of being gay but to anyone who has suffered for simply being different.

Love and peace to you all.
Allan Macintyre Clark

In our lifetimes, it seems that the instances when people are suffering visibly the torment of pain, sadness and sorrow, it more easily brings out the sympathy, the empathy of others. It shows that as humans, we have the power to love. We take on the qualities, the abilities that are inherent to our existence that unite as one race. Even those of us who are marginalised in life are more easily accepted by those who marginalise through our suffering. Even if it is not shown outwardly, there is created an inner sense of remorse. It allows, if you will, humanity to reach out. And for however long, in most instances not for very long at all, the vast majority find the love for another no matter what their circumstance.

Wouldn't it be amazing if somehow, once love is found under those circumstances, it would be everlasting? On the flip side, ironically, if those who are marginalised learn to embrace who they are and want to celebrate the love they have found for themselves, for their truths, they are ridiculed, chastised, taunted, even harmed physically in many instances. Why then is it so difficult for those who marginalise others to celebrate, to love, even if only to sympathise when joy and happiness is expressed. Why is it easier to express your humanity to others when they are crying out loud about their suffering rather than when they are celebrating the joy of accepting who they are as a person equal to any other?

One

Ode to those higher up

Standing in a bar with complete anonymity,
Trying to escape the complicated proximity
Of a world full of controversy,
And the perils that it brings when one simply wants nothing more than harmony.
Having to deal with a culture based on deceit, and a hidden agenda.
Why place so much importance on being that transparent pretender?
Please don't try to hide what is so obviously clear,
It does nothing with all that I've learned to endure,
The respect that you obviously crave in instilling fear.
I try to conform with all of my heart,
Compromising my values in doing my part,
To all those above me who desperately need
The self-justification on which they feed,
It will never cease to amaze me in the obvious and predictable plan
How everyone whose sole objective is to gain the upper hand,
when the more compassionate route would simply be to understand.

Why not place your faith and trust in those who are truly committed to meeting demands?
It is always apparent, at least in my mind's eye,
With whom I can most often completely rely,
And if anytime there is ever a question, I would offer all of my clout
To give them every benefit of any doubt.
For that is what matters day in and day out
To retain the loyalty and the respect of those whose passion is what its really all about.

Two

Ratatouille

Do you remember that first time we met?
It was then so blissful, now one I'll always regret.
Staring across that crowded bar never was I so taken in
By that face, those eyes that playful grin,
You were there with a dear friend, Tina was her name
It was a thrill watching you play the game,
Having the confidence of being with one so dear
For me, alone, I'm sure that wasn't as obviously clear.
I can't recall entirely, but I believe at one point you invited me over.
What ensued was amazing banter so poignant, so clever.
I'll never forget what came over me during our conversation,
All the joy that flooded my head surging with no reservation,
The excitement seemed to grow with each passing moment,
Never would I have imagined how much I would lament, even after all these years how I suffer such pain, sorrow and torment.
In looking back at that fateful day,
When you and I seemed to have so much in common.
Never would I think how badly you would betray

All the faith that I had at the time in love and
a forever union
It is so difficult for me to revisit
The very moment you spoke of such wonderful things,
like your recipe.
whose secret ingredient the caper made the perfect
ratatouille.
You captured my imagination, my heart, my belief
As I recall I was filled with such a sense of relief
That my quest to find my perfect Ken doll
had ended without having faced any big fall.
And remembering what we had,
I couldn't have been any more naïve.
How I wish I had been more discerning and had the
courage to leave.
For all the signs were there for so long,
I chose to ignore them desperately hoping
I was terribly wrong.
I would like to find a reason for all of this sadness,
Unfortunately, it will forever remain my era of
complete madness.

Three

What big shoes seemingly

Who will buy my love now on sale?
A bargain for very little, guaranteed never to fail.
The price one will pay has no monetary value,
The only requirement is to be treated with the gentleness it is due.
This love of mine has been abused
By some who seemed in the end quite amused
And by others who really hadn't a clue.
I'm not looking for anyone's sympathy,
All right perhaps a bit of empathy,
But I'm fully aware that my plight not unique to others,
However, certainly something I would like vindicated if I had my druthers.
When I was young, I never imagined that while searching for love I would stumble and fall,
Never able to stand fully, never getting past the first step of learning to crawl.
As a result, it seems that I have lost any confidence
In my ability to connect to another given
any circumstance.
I wander through this life giving my search for love such high importance,

Knowing in my heart at the end of the day it is of such little consequence.
What is the answer I ask myself so much of the time?
To that end, my search always constant but thus far nowhere near sublime.
Wherever there has been any initial joy
It has been fleeting like playing with an unwanted Christmas toy.
Perhaps with all that has come to pass,
There is a silver lining that has surrounded this seemingly dark cloud alas,
For the hurt, anger and pain that I once allowed to consume me,
Has no longer the effect that then crippled all of my ability
So when I say that my love is for sale, take heed
Make sure that you understand fully this breed
For it requires a very special skill
A combination of understanding, tolerance and long-lasting commitment.
Are those shoes the right size for you to fill?

Four

Sunbathed fields

Who is this man? I ask myself
causing me a sleepless night in bed.
Just one of so many questions that are, at this moment, swirling in my head.
A man with eyes so deep in colour
like staring into a dark abyss of endless wonder.
After our very brief encounter today,
I left his company feeling a bit cheated although much to my delight he wasted little time to say
That it was always his intention to tease and happily I let go the haunting feeling of dismay.
I remember saying to him that this is proving to be a very good time in my life,
A period seemingly filled with an unusual run of good fortune, perhaps an end to all my past strife?
True to form, I allowed myself to believe that nothing would come of what is again a projection of fantasy
And reality would clearly win out once more continuing what I have unceasingly proclaimed to be my destiny.
Ironically, there is a calmness within
whispering perhaps I should allow myself this opportunity to grow with him.

For after so many years of coming out on the losing end
Perhaps I will finally register a win.
So all that remains for me to say,
is that my hope continues to be eternal,
in seeing me finally reach those sunbathed fields so abundantly fertile.

Five

Why is it that I always end up haunted?

Why is it that I always end up haunted
By the only thing I've ever wanted?
Why has it come to be that hearing the words which once meant everything to me
Now seem empty and with a total lack of honesty?
Whenever they are uttered
It's as if they are only muttered
As if they lack the intensity, or worse, of having the propensity
Of what I expect a person to feel for me.
Is he the man of my dreams?
An unfortunate recurring theme.
That seems to enter into my head just after we've gone to bed
The energy that ensues
Trying to convince myself
That all those exaggerated clues
Only end up being
what I ultimately see as nothing more than wishful thinking
Those precious words of which I have just spoken
Will forever mean nothing more than a simple token

of one's appreciation
and ending there without reciprocation.
For this final attempt on my part
To believe in the power of "I love you" has for the last time broken my heart.

Six

The attraction was there

The attraction was there from the very start
So strong it was like magnets whose force unable to be pulled apart.
That face, that smile, those eyes, that look,
How could I resist?
What else could I possibly do but allow you to persist?
Those glances back and forth which ensued
Were nothing less than the thrill of being pursued,
Like animals on a mission
To attain that final position.
On those occasions that are limited by time
The result no less than sublime.
As time has passed from that initial meeting
I have grown to love you more despite all
the bickering
Your constant attempt to make it known that you are your own independent man
I've never been fooled in the least
Bound and determined to tame that beast.
I know you love me and you always will
In spite of all those efforts to fill
My head with cruelty, often a very bitter pill.
I love you and I always will.

You can fight what we both feel for each other and you can blame me for the bogus negativity,
But in the end you are your own worst enemy.
And with all that you've said throughout our plight
I will finally set my sight
On the contentment I finally feel
knowing that this attraction of ours has always been very real
Wherever I may go to now, whether near or far will I vow
To always have hope that you and I
Will in the end be able to cry
"We will never again be apart
As the love we share is bonded from the heart."

Seven

A love of which cannot be spoken

A love undeniably more than just a token
Of all my feelings for you must be real
in a world who dismisses them
as nothing more than sin,
however, they chose to deny
what is mine will never rely
On those who refuse to admit
what to them can never be legit.
But for me I will not allow any naysayer to dictate
What is or is not my fate.
As dusk settles on my life,
I feel as though I have been given one last chance
to end the strife.
That which has taken from me
all the joy that is the biggest part of living,
God has it been a long time coming.
The end that I have been able to express
All the sentiments that in the past
have never been allowed to last.
My heart once again full of hope
that perhaps the possibility will finally prevail
to bring about the inner peace
which will instill once and for evermore

that my love for you and yours for me will prevail
and endure from our hearts to our very core.

Eight

Transparent as glass

You say you want to love me,
How can I take this seriously when truly you don't?
Like those from your mouth many words can be
fleeting, so believe them I won't.

It's so easy to say what you think others want to hear
When you carelessly believe it's so obviously clear.
Unfortunately, there are those whose paths you will
cross
calling your intentions transparent as glass.

I have so often been exposed to the games people play
making it near impossible to believe the words they say.
Please don't reveal your ignorance any further
for it will only make it harder with anything else you
mutter.

It's so easy to say, what you think others want to hear
When you carelessly believe it's so obviously clear.
Unfortunately, there are those whose paths you will
cross calling your intentions transparent as glass.

It's time that you learn being true to yourself
and exposing those feelings you want me to address
will certainly make it much easier to accept
the love with which you want to impress.

It's so easy to say, what you think others want to hear
When you carelessly believe it's so obviously clear.
Unfortunately, there are those whose paths you will
cross calling your intentions transparent as glass.

One day that man will come along,
the one to realise it's very simple indeed.
Love me from the deepest place in your heart,
Put all your trust in us and we will never part,
that is my creed.

It's so easy to say what you think others want to hear
When you carelessly believe it's so obviously clear.
Unfortunately, there are those whose paths you will
cross calling your intentions transparent as glass.

Nine

For all of us who have suffered

In a world where we all strive to find our place
It is unfortunate how many obstacles we must face.
Constantly challenged by those who don't have a clue
But eventually the day will come that they rue
All the times having selfishly contributed
To the stress, pain and anguish for which we have attributed,
our eventual lack of faith in mankind,
From those whose intentions are so completely blind
Where is the love, we constantly ask ourselves?
One of the easiest emotions to summon from our mind's pantry of shelves
Filled with all that we attain in acquiring life's common knowledge
A virtual degree in humanity far beyond the grounds of any college.
It is a concoction mixed with common sense that releases our ability
to let go of what others expect from us in order to advance their own stability.
I will never give in to the ridiculous notion
that those who think they hold higher positions in life have the right to set in motion

Their overzealous acts of cruelty and torment,
Leaving all of us who are caring to lament
The tragedies these cowards have gone to such
lengths to create.
Whose sole intention is to break our hearts and deflate
The only thing in this life that can bring
humanity together
The one emotion that will sit so peacefully on that shelf
in the pantry.
Forever and ever.

Ten

Sunken Treasure

When sadness builds from a place of strength
It seems that life is a struggle at any length
that I have chosen to go to improve upon that emotion,
Never seeming to stir more than a bit of commotion.
The end result that I manage to face
Is the realisation of the enormity of commitment it will take to erase
All the pain and suffering that has denied my life pleasure
And robbed me of the wonderful treasure
That I set out to find with such strong convictions
With optimism, eagerness and amazing expectations.
Now I look back with anger and pain,
Having nothing more than complete disdain
For all those who have felt the need to thwart my journey
And cause me to struggle for what seems an endless eternity
How can I reverse the terrible wrongs at this point?
At my age
And harness the power that fills my head with rage
Allowing me the energy to turn my life's direction,
once and for all

Giving me the opportunity to stand firm and tall
And look at those who have preyed upon my
generosity of spirit,
And my eagerness to always give strength and merit
To those who are deserving of the chances that
have passed me by
Robbed of opportunities that I have created to simply
try
To live a life free from the torment that people seem
to gain pleasure
Refusing to allow me that ever elusive treasure.

Eleven

Pretending to be in love

He stole my heart
Understanding all along that we would one day part
And played me for a fool.
How can anyone knowingly be so cruel?
Pretending to enjoy a journey of monumental importance
Never truly realising the devastating consequence
Of the actions of a man at no time truly engaged,
Treating me like an animal whose life has been caged.
In the end making it feel
So wickedly surreal
How clever he was never to let on
While roaming the streets looking for others to prey upon.
Carefully using the time that we were apart
To satisfy the urges that replaced his emptiness present from the very start.
I will always be in a state of shock
At the ease with which he did mock
The true love that I felt for this seemingly, wonderful man
And the number of years this game he played did span
I have to admit with a great deal of discomfort

How impressed I am now with such premeditated effort,
For it shows me the lengths to which one will endeavour
And the lack of respect it must summon to think it so clever
To deceive oneself and all those around him
And to believe that this view of life so grim
Would not one day come back to haunt his twisted mind
And invoke pity from all those he once thought so blind.
I revel now in the wisdom that I gained from this permanently scarred experience
And the hope that in the grand scheme of my life it will turn out to be of little consequence.

Twelve

A tribute to my dear friends and family

You are my towering fortress
my unwavering strength and prowess.
My beacon of light through the darkness
That so often blankets my ability to harness
the power of all my potential,
A gift I've been given by no means unsubstantial.
And though we are now so many miles apart
I love you more with all my heart.
For it is your patience, comfort and understanding
which allows me to face what seems a
constant battering.
Driving me to continue this journey, so demanding
Of the energy it takes just to remain standing.
I think about you each and every day
wondering often what it is you would say.
In answering the quandaries that are so often perplexing
and the lack of consideration which is disturbingly distracting.
Thankfully, whenever it all becomes too much for me to process,
You are always there to relieve the terrible stress
That rears its ugly face to manipulate

The calm to which you insist I capitulate.
And think about all that I have managed to accomplish
And let go of the poison that is produced to diminish
the amazing life that I have been able to lead,
Surely more than enough to supersede
All the doubt that poison would allow to fester
If not for the encouragement you constantly muster
To reel in all my self-deprecating tendencies to
which I am prone,
By pointing out that no matter how often I feel alone
You will always be there with undying support
To prop me back up so that I will never abort.
The dreams that I have always seen as viable
And with the tools I have been given absolutely
achievable.
So to this end I say, without any hesitation and from
the depths of my soul
Thank you for taking on so selflessly such a difficult
role.

Thirteen

Another lonely day

For all of us having suffered
The indignation of a lover
Who has selfishly put us through the sorrow,
Never thinking about the weeks, the months that may follow
with all the torment of trying to understand
What went wrong with the life that was planned
Sharing the trust that we both supposedly craved
And the commitment about which we so eagerly raved
To that end with all my heart I would like to say
As the sun rises on yet another lonely day,
I write all of these words with the hope that it will help to resolve
Any lack of faith that may have evolved
From the indiscretions and lack of integrity
Of those whose selfish impropriety
Would have never reared its ugly face
At a time that anyone would embrace
The wound that would cut our lives so deep
And leave our hearts to do nothing but weep
For all of the precious time that seemed wasted
On a dream that was so cruelly lambasted
By the one person who in our mind was above

Any act that would destroy the deep love
Never believing that from the very start,
His motivations would eventually drive us apart.
If only his true feelings from the beginning would have been made clear,
The hurt that was suffered would never have come so horribly near,
To destroying all that we held in the highest esteem
Never believing for a single second he could end our most precious dream.

Fourteen

Streams of tears cascading down my face

Streams of tears cascading down my face
Evident of more than just a perpetual trace
Of a love continually sought after
Undying and absolute, that is what I have to offer
Never happy with being resolute
I'd rather face the longest commute
To find that man who would recognise
The difficult journey so evident in the pools of these blue eyes.
Why are people so quick to judge?
Never able to process the difficult realisation
That accompany determined and
unwavering resolutions
trying to discover that elusive but understanding mind
In what seems as I age an impossible find.
I hope and pray
With each passing day
That all this turmoil will at long last
Be erased or at the very least reconciled from this torturous past.
The inspiration which haunts me to compose these words
Raises its ugly face once again

When I am reminded of all the pain
That I suffer on each occasion
The curse of my elusive expectation.

Fifteen

I'm almost home

My Scotland what she means to me
From walking her ancient streets in the capital
To the paths around lovely villages like Pitlochry.
Wherever I seem to go within her amazing borders, I feel a spirit, a sense of pride, a deep history.
From a young lad who could never wait to return
To see the family and place for which I yearned
I remember so much of the times that I spent at my grandparents' home.
The senses of comfort and joy abounded, never feeling alone.
As I grew older, the desire to be there
Became stronger and more difficult to bare
The separation that has gone on far too long
Which will soon be a part of my history righting an overdue wrong.
What drives my attraction to this country
is something far beyond its natural beauty,
It lies in the emotion that comes from within
A place in the heart where love plays to win.
I've travelled the world and have seen much beauty
But none that can match that of "auld reekie."
And if one were to measure the spirit

Of the Scots that exists
There would ne'er be a visitor who could resist
That which I have known from the depths of my being
And it's for this reason that I am finally seeing,
Why in my lifetime I have gone to extremes
Trying to find the answers when they've always been there in my dreams
Of residing in the solace to which I've always been drawn
To the land, to its people and to my family, that is where
I truly belong.

Sixteen

Ode to an unrequited love

All the things that I say
Come from the depths wherein my feelings lay,
Bringing them to the surface, a task made simple when
I feel that the person would be open to each and
every one of them
Many mistakes I have indeed made
At which point those emotions will quickly fade
Back into those depths where the wounds go to heal
Readying my heart for yet another attempt to feel
the love and desire I so desperately crave
Until that happens acting outwardly brave.
Yes, there are times out of complete despair,
I turn to those with whom I abandon all care
And take the risks that come with that unfortunate
frame of mind,
Feigning the pleasure as if completely blind
Having met the man who I believe is of my dreams
Has caused me now what it seems
A bevy of anxieties that question the possibility
Of things going wrong through my mind's negativity.
So far, happily, this man has been more than supportive
Towards all those thoughts that can be so corrosive

To a relationship that begins with eagerness and promise
More often than not ending up in by now a familiar abyss
Once again I hope and pray
With the passing of each day
That this man will be there for me in the end
And with his love and devotion help to mend
The many years of terrible doubt
and lack of confidence of which I now seem to constantly write about.

Seventeen

The path all too recognisable

My life's journey again continues on its recognisable path
Having veered off course momentarily now back with familiar wrath.
Once more it seems that this person's ability to be honest and true,
Has fallen to the wayside, never really having had a clue.
It's terrible to assume that how someone behaves at the start
Is an indication of how he feels in his heart,
And unfortunately, the scepticism created in my mind
Is pushing me to become completely blind.
To all the signs that would normally tell someone to stay away
Keeping my feelings to myself, completely at bay.
Unfortunately for me, as is evident in my past,
My heart has been an open book, apparently a detriment to finding love that will last.
I suppose that if I were to start over again,
Knowing what I know now I would keep hidden my Feelings, avoiding the pain
That has reared its ugly face one too many a time
And has taken away the joy of romance, an experience meant to be so sublime.

But for now, in the autumn of my life I have no desire to change,
For it would take far too much effort to rearrange
The core beliefs that I have followed for all of my life,
Those which have caused me so much strife
I will continue on this path of which I speak
And pray that one day soon a love will appear that will be mine to keep,
And the joy that we will share from that day forward
Will mend forever all that pain and allow to move toward
The end of my life with no more regret
For the wasted time that it will have taken me to finally forget
The dishonesty and fear displayed by all the others
Finally meeting the one fearless in his ability to give back the love, I will then have achieved my druthers.

Eighteen

A clever disguise

In a world that has proven to cause me so much pain
The love you have given thus far is as soothing as Novocain.
How long it will last, I have no idea
For it is at this point far from any assured panacea.
Particularly when the pain runs so deep,
As I know far too well when it wears off I will again weep.
I pray each day that what you offer
will go a long way
in mending the extensive decay
That seems to have taken hold
of the dream that was once as precious to me as gold.
How long will you be able to maintain
What it would take to sustain
The commitment of which I have always wanted
in return for the love that I would gladly give undaunted?
Why can I not feel assured that you are in my life to stay?
Why is my enthusiasm always taken in the wrong way?
Is it so wrong to believe that what we all want is to find in the end?

That safe place where all the tools are there that it takes to mend.
All the hope that has been shattered,
All the dreams that have been battered,
And finally, with the help of God's good grace
Those painful experiences will be all but completely erased
And what difference I can only imagine it will make how we finally get to that place
At what seems to have been slower than a snail's meandering pace.

Nineteen

Peace of mind

I've endured so much heartache in my lifetime,
Causing my emotions to spin constantly on a dime.
One day my head is high above the clouds,
The next I find myself in darkness crying out loud,
I yearn to get to that place where I am at peace within my mind,
Where no one can hurt me from being so unkind.
The journey that has taken me on this treacherous path
Leaving me alone to deal with my wrath
And the sorrow which follows all the pain that has occurred
Consuming my world with the disappointment I have suffered.
What is the answer, where can it be found?
On this path to uncertainty and disappointment, why am I bound?
Have I not faced enough of life's difficult tests?
What will it take to finally achieve my quest?
I've never asked a lot of the men who I have embraced
When will the memories of all these naïve choices be effaced?
This story seems to play over and over again in my mind.

How can I continue to be so blind?
What kind of desperation does it take
To suffer repeatedly every choice that I make?
Enough already! Please leave me in peace,
I'm tired and now begging that this pain finally cease.
How much longer must my emotions face this
constant barrage?
Finding true love in a good man seems as fleeting as a
desert mirage.
I lay in my bed almost every night,
Consumed with frustration and the horrible fright
Of never having again a peaceful night's sleep.
Alone with no man at my side I will forever weep
With the constant fear that he simply doesn't exist
Leaving me doomed to live the rest of my life in this
lonely abyss.
Tossing and turning,
my brain constantly working,
Desperate to find that place in my mind
Where I can go to one night finally find
Where there is calm and true happiness in my solace
Where I will finally have what we all need to achieve
within ourselves peace.

Twenty

Has the dark cloud gone away?

The dark cloud that has been following me wherever I go
Was dispersed finally with the force of an unrelenting foe.
I looked into his eyes and I knew straight away
that this would be a life changing day.
Having spent less than a week sending texts back and forth
My mind wasted no time recognising his worth,
The calmness of his demeanor,
The softness of his voice
To have those qualities I would gladly pay any price.
I couldn't stop gazing into those eyes
As radiant as star sapphires,
as powerful as my heart's desires
Fast forward and once again what I saw was nothing more than a dream
I awaken to realise that nothing has changed from the old familiar theme
How I continue to be smitten
By the impressions with which I am so easily stricken
Will never cease to amaze.

As I should by now know that it's nothing more than a haze Inevitably being lifted
As the questions that I ask myself are sifted
And the true colours of the person ever forming in my mind
Are eventually allowed to shine,
Showing me that what I thought to be blissful
Was nothing more than regretful
For having again wasted the time
On the possibility of love, in reality, far from sublime.
So here I am, ready to pen
These familiar words that flood my head once again
Like a boxer who refuses to buckle under constant blows to the head,
I continue to torture myself with these feelings I should by now truly dread.
How much longer can these dark clouds continue to appear?
Before all the faith in love that I initially had disappears.
I hold on to that notion now by an ever-fraying rope
With each and every day that passes less and less hope
That the love of my life still waits just beyond all
this sorrow
And maybe holding on to my dream he will appear tomorrow.

Twenty-one

The indignity of it all

Pain, torment, sorrow and bullied are all that we feel
When the day finally dawns that who we are is undeniably real.
Having to admit to ourselves we are gay,
Knowing what we face, the incessant accusations that we have been led astray.
The years that pass of facing frequent consternation
The indignity, the cruelty and the total humiliation
From family, school kids, neighbours and colleagues we experience,
Until we are forced to lash out or retreat, into total defiance
Why does this world seem to fascinate
In its ability to assassinate
The self-worth of those who appear different to them
Happy in the process to invoke hate and to create mayhem.
It was easier although no less forgivable in the past,
For humanity had far fewer causes to lambast
But today, there are so many more where the focus should lie
Cruelty to others who are simply trying to get by.

In a world where we all struggle against poverty, inequality, pollution, and greed to name just a few,
Why do people support those who really haven't a clue?
By turning a blind eye to those who lack real compassion
Is only allowing them their unfounded aggression.
It is said that God created man in his own image
I'm afraid that I must challenge that old adage
As unfortunate as it is impossible to believe,
For if he would have given every man equal ability to rationalise and comprehend
There would never be cause thus the need to offend
And man would be left to face the simple task of living in harmony wouldn't that be sublime
With his only concern to leave it in the peaceful state with which it had been maintained throughout time.

Twenty-two

Past the point of no return

I sit in my room each night before I sleep
Fighting back the tears and the strong urge I have to weep.
Listening to songs whose lyrics flood my mind with the sad
memories in my past
Wondering how long these reminders will continue to torment, continue to last.
It is a battle that has been waged for such a long time,
To the point when I must very soon draw the line,
For if I continue to allow this pain to linger on
Then any chance for me to salvage some happiness
will soon be gone.
Time is now my enemy and with each passing day
it only gets stronger,
The very reason why I can delay no longer.
Somebody show me the strength, and the courage to continue this journey,
Give me a sign why I have expended so much energy
Will in the end I have the outcome for which I have
been yearning?
My reward for what has been a never-ending curve of learning.

I can only forge ahead on this path for which I have chosen
Having past that point
In my life of no return that is for certain,
So, I will plod along continuing to hope,
Begging for a result that will allow me to finally cope,
With all the anguish that has filled my life up to now
Praying to the powers that be to finally allow
All those dreams that have plagued my past with dismay
Coming to the resolution that will finally allow me to say
Welcome to my world, take your coat off,
and for the time I have left plan to stay.

Twenty-three

What is the meaning of love?

What is the meaning of love?
The search for which I've had enough,
The time I've spent trying to find it
Has given me nothing but the desire to quit
I've looked high and low all my life it seems
To satisfy all of those naive dreams.
That I had when I was young
To find that man who would become,
The answer to that elusive question,
Which seemingly eludes any real definition.
And has, thus far, failed all of my intuition
The number of men who have paraded through my life
Causing me in the end nothing but pain and strife.
Promising that their intentions were completely true
Only for me to find out when we were through
That their motives were completely self-serving.
What have I done to be so deserving?
It seems that I must have done something terrible in the past
For this pattern of hurt continues to last
From one disappointment to the next
Giving my story a resounding pretext
Of falling in love to no avail

Never the ending that I once imagined would prevail.
How can I turn this treacherous tide?
Will there ever be that man to whom
I may confide?
And finally feel that he will be there to listen,
To nurture, to comfort with no ulterior mission
But to let me know that nothing I will ever do or say,
Will allow his feelings for me to sway.
For the attraction that he has for me comes from deep
within
And will never allow him to give in
Like it has with all the others in my past
Only then will I know that our love stands
the chance to truly last.

Twenty-four

Escape from reality

Escape the day, escape the pain,
Breathe in and feel all that you gain
It's so easy, it's so satisfying
It allows your focus to be about pleasure and all things gratifying.
When the crippling power of sadness, anger and frustration, permeates your entire being to the point of desperation,
Breathe in and feel how all your troubles seem to disappear,
All your concerns no longer strike fear.
However, knowing your limitations is the definitive rule,
Failure to do so will only leave you the fool
For the euphoria that one feels is so tempting to assimilate
That is when all senses of reality become impossible to regulate.
It is a state of mind of which one must always be cautious
Considering how much of the lives of so many leave them nauseous.
Crossing the line too often and succumbing to the euphoric bliss,
The path back to normalcy will become easier and easier to miss.

I have always been fortunate never having lost complete sight of reality
And become a statistic of desperation to end the pain of a troubled life with another fatality.
Whatever may end up being the cause of an early departure,
Has been well worth the many times when I needed to feel some rapture.
For all that I have had to deal with, the emotional and psychological trauma
I have turned to self-induced exhilaration in order to remove myself from my life's drama.
Whatever may transpire with the limited time that exists,
I will continue to do what I have done in the past to resist
the emotions that constantly bring me down,
That make me feel like the sad circus clown.
Never losing sight that one day I will witness a dramatic shift,
And finally, realise the end of a life gone adrift.

Twenty-five

Life comes and life goes

Life comes and life goes.
Having said that it is important that one knows
The challenges that we all encounter on a daily basis
Are individually not worthy of the regard we place on them and how they're seemingly thrust upon us,
Like paint on a canvass they are all only clues to the final picture
And indications to how our lives can take on a positive or negative structure.
As relevant as they may seem at the time,
Giving these individual challenges too much
importance would be in the end a terrible crime.
Instead, perhaps look upon them like a loving parent to a new born child feeling the need to nurture.
That perhaps is the key for having a more successful future,
We all struggle, and for the desperate, it seems like a daily battle
Constantly testing our resolve and causing our nerves to continually rattle.
It is for those individuals where my sympathy lies as I have been one
Where the heart and the soul feel like a loaded gun.

Ready to go off on any given day
Hoping against hope many times that it will never happen we pray.
It is to those people alone, that I beg never give in,
For the successful journey one travels getting through each and every day is the ultimate win.
So remember, in life look at the journey as a nurturing parent trying to give a child's life structure
Individual successes and failure are unimportant and only paint on canvas which in the end will reveal that amazing picture.

Twenty-six

Just another typical holiday season

Another holiday season is fast approaching
And it looks like it will again be typically encroaching
On a life that is filled with unhappiness for most of the rest of the year,
Wouldn't it be a relief if instead it was filled with Christmas cheer?
Checking out from the drama of a lonely and disappointing existence
And perhaps enjoying the splendour of all the pomp and pretence,
I suppose if I were given a time to relax and forget about all my troubles,
I would choose, like many, this season of chocolate, caviar and bubbles.
It is unfortunate that a time of year which is supposed to allow us to celebrate the wonders of humanity,
Instead has only ended up emphasising our struggles with sadness and depravity.
And when all is said and done
with promises of new beginnings and a happier year to come
By now my faith in the possibility of better times has fallen on deaf ear and left me numb.

Hope springs eternal or so it is said
For me, hope is all that keeps me from my eternal bed
I would never wish the disappointment that has plagued my life on another,
For even in those brief periods when it would look like I may perhaps recover
I'm looking ahead at the time when what I have known will return with fervent indignation,
Leaving what I thought may be the end of my darkness a mere figment of my imagination.
Having said all that, I have just said I so want in spite of what may be perceived as irreversible
To say to all those that have endured their own living hell that I truly believe nothing is impossible,
And if it means that I wake up dreading what may derail any chance of happiness each day,
I will do it knowing that I have, if nothing else, the inner strength to hold this cruelty at bay.
It's as if I want to express that whatever spanner is thrown to prevent me from achieving once and for all the happiness that I fought for so very long,
Will never alter my resolve for ending my pursuit now, so late in this game would be very wrong!

Twenty-seven

How we suffer in vain

There is no cause for alarm
For an event like this is not meant to harm
But simply an attempt from those we hold so dear
To let us know that life is not about having this love forever here
What a luxury it has been to have them in our lives
And then, without warning, that comfort becomes seemingly unfair as it dies
Fear not, I know it appears as though you have been abandoned,
With all the joy that you knew having been remanded.
All that love you have known from he who you held so dear,
Has suddenly and without warning pushed you into a place of fear.
There is a message from those we cherish who leave us to fend for ourselves,
That dependency on another, for now, might better sit on a back shelf.
Think about it, would that not allow the focus to be placed on our own dream,
If only to help ease the pain in the loss of he who was held in such high esteem.

In the end when one is able to continue their own journey while here on this earth,
We will one day look upon our dearly departed as we march forth.
With his love in our heart and his passion in our heads, we will finally understand
That all the joy and support that was bestowed upon us while he was at hand.
Is actually cause for celebration not fear
and warrants the fervour of our greatest cheer.

Twenty-eight

To what am I referring!

It was never so easy, it was never so clear
It was always something I wanted to hear
It was all that I hung onto, it was all that I yearned for,
It was all of which I ever wanted and more.
Such a basic need, so satisfying when it comes your way
And yet so fleeting if you keep it at bay.
When I look back at the many opportunities to have what I hold so dear,
I'll never understand why I only managed to get so near
To that elusive but not uncommon dream.
Something I continue to hold in such high esteem
Always optimistic so I suppose I will forever cling
To the joy and the ecstasy that it will one day bring.
How many chances in one lifetime are handed?
For a person to seize the big prize before he is branded,
Always the best man and never the groom
How unfortunate, how sad having to face that doom and gloom.
I cannot be accused of not putting myself out there
For one only needs to look at the scars my heart has had to bare
It is the chances that I have chosen to take
And I suppose those choices I will continue to make.

Until that day when it will cease to be an enigmatic belief
That this dream of falling in love will arrive at my doorstep, bringing with it monumental and glorious relief.

Twenty-nine

The End

Life is certainly full of ups and downs
But I believe the measure of its success is in how a person rebounds.
The ups are certainly very easy to take
But only teach us that to rely on their ever presence is a big mistake.
It is a testament to our longevity and resilience
How we handle the downs, the true indication of human brilliance.
For those are the times in our lives when we are faced with the important questions,
And given the opportunities to make the right choices through heartfelt and intelligent reflections.
They teach us that perhaps a change in direction would be worthwhile,
For the path on which we are travelling may be pot marked with too much denial.
As another year of introspection comes to a close,
I look towards the new one with positivity and excitement to see how it all goes.
For the first time, in more years than I care to remember,
I will leave all my pain, anxiety and turmoil with this last day of December.

The excitement within can hardly be contained
As I can finally look forward with peace in my heart finally attained.
Knowing that there is true love and positive changes on the horizon
And with that amazing challenges to which I can finally focus all my attention.

Thirty

My inspiration from chatting to Jane

They say that practice makes perfect, they say that time heals all wounds,
I say that when you trust in yourself those former thoughts will then become truths.
The journey to that realisation may be long, sometimes seemingly endless,
But continue the pursuit and I promise the power from that positivity you will harness.
I know there will be moments when you feel you can go on no longer,
Please re-read these words that I write and you will again become stronger.
The pain that I have suffered, many times self-inflicted
Has prevented me from moving forward, feeling that all I do is self-inhibited.
But I can say with the strength of all who have been in my circle
That what I have finally achieved seems nothing less than a true miracle,
And now all that remains is for me to share this gift
For I am truly aware of what it means to have lived a life gone adrift.
With what I have gone through over all of my years,

There is nothing more that can be thrown at me which will insight any more fears.
My path has now been cleared for me to achieve peace and satisfaction in whatever I may attempt,
To that point when things don't go as planned, no matter, I will feel no contempt.
For in life we should always be made very clearly aware,
That to try anything, even if it brings failure, there is no cause for despair.
Look upon each and every attempt that you make in your life,
As one less pursuit that you will have to attempt as you strive
To come to the conclusion that to wherever your journey may end,
It is the process that you can proudly defend.
To any naysayer and that includes your own self-doubts,
You have the power within to make that which you have achieved no matter how seemingly insignificant, the ultimate turnabout.

Thirty-one

What took me so long!

When you feel down as if life is constantly kicking you in the teeth,
Look up and quickly notice from where you are lying beneath
that ugly face you see as your life taking pleasure
In all of your failures with sadistic and calculated measure.
Notice how all of its movement seems to mimic
All the gestures you make perhaps that might prove prolific.
I know at those times when staring at your life's ugly side
You feel as if there's no alternative but to cry
Having been there so many, many times in my past
I am here to tell you with hope in your heart these terrible feelings will not last.
And also this, I am here to say, has come all to light very recently
My God, how long it has taken to finally break free
Of those painful clutches that have limited my movement
So much energy, anguish and time has been spent
Seemingly wasted on something to many others that is so obvious.

What they don't understand is that their lives are not yours, for that they are oblivious.
Look again and stare straight into those eyes of that ugly face, do you not see something very similar?
If you look hard enough, I think perhaps there may be something that seems quite familiar.
If not, then fear not, for that day will come when you will realise
And you will understand with a smile there was no compromise.
In attaining that freedom your heart will overflow with rapture,
That your eyes have finally been able to capture
The ugly face of what seemed your downtrodden life
Was but a mere reflection of your own face brought on by years of strife.
Now with all that knowledge and wisdom on file,
Look again at that ugly face with your biggest smile
And notice now what is staring at you from above
How extraordinary, a face with that same smile,
draw your own conclusions, my love!

Thirty-two

Vindication

At a time of the year that traditionally has caused me no end of despair
I must vow to myself to try earnestly to repair
The accumulation of grief and bad memories of seasons gone by,
Those that have clouded my vision and limited my ability to enjoy
The opportunity that affords all of us the chance to rise above
All of our anxieties, hostilities and inability to love.
It is so easy to fall into that self-deprecating pattern,
That in the end only adds to sadness that I, for one, seem to constantly yearn.
Break free, grab the lion by its mane
And do what might seem unnatural, attempt to start again,
Show all those that have created in you such effacing self-doubt.
It is in our power to remove all the stains that discolour our life's grout.
To once and for all, tell all the naysayers in my head,
It's time to put all the shame, all the pain to bed
Use all that you have learned, all that you know to be true

All the knowledge and wisdom that you have been able to accrue,
And move forward with the strength and conviction
That from the very beginning gave you the hope and anticipation
Of a rich and fulfilling life abundant with good times, good friendships
And the dream of finding that one perfect relationship.
As I sit alone, observing all the people around me
Seeing the many smiling faces and jolly laughter, appearing to be free
Of all that burdensome baggage that seems to constantly weigh me down.
I think to myself that perhaps now is the time to send in the clowns,
And once and for all say "stop" to this dizzying merry-go-round
That has for much too long limited my choices and managed to confound
The thoughts I once had of a world that had no bounds
That the talent with which I have been blessed
Will in the end be more than enough to impress
The biggest critic who has allowed this negativity
to exist for so long.
Yes, it's time to look in the mirror and finally understand
that I can let it all go, that I do, indeed, belong.

Thirty-three

Are you really in love?

Disagreements are created for us to rise above
The occasions that question our devotion, that test our love.
In a world so fast paced, it would be very naïve
To consider that everyone in our lives would perceive
That every situation happening on a daily basis
Would never insight anger, sadness or disappointment from within us.
For selflessness to occur at every turn
Certainly something we all should yearn,
Tis but an occurrence that would only happen in a perfect world,
The reality is that selfishness is more often the face in life unfurled.
Any loss that comes about, any time we feel wronged,
The focus is always on how we are affected, thus, the healing is always prolonged.
We wallow in self-pity, laying blame on all the others
When in fact, perhaps we should all be looking in our respective mirrors.
Surely, true love should allow us all to rise above any inconveniences,

Proving that we are prepared to look beyond those insignificant consequences.
That at the end of the day is more an indication
Of the lengths we are prepared to go to prove our devotion,
And say to the most significant person in our lives
"Do not worry, my love, your troubles are my own, with my help you will survive."

Thirty-four

What is Commitment?

Commitment, what a wonderful notion.
For people who love, there is no stronger potion.
It is a bond that by definition should never be broken
It is a bilateral pact never to be forsaken.
A word not to be taken lightly
For it encompasses the strength of one's integrity.
It is not, however, achieved without constant dedication
It requires a lifetime of undivided attention.
Approach it always with energy and passion
Words these days which have fallen out of fashion.
But rewarded in the end with comfort, love and companionship,
Without which we face a lifetime of loneliness and hardship.
A concept that is truly irreplaceable
For the benefits that we feel are without any doubt undeniable.
Through time we learn of its value
And the mistakes that we make give us the clue
That to forsake ourselves this gift given to us from above
Would be choosing to discount the power of love.
It is shameful in this age of turmoil and strife

That humanity has lost this will to commit,
surely the answer to a peaceful life.

Thirty-five

The forever love in my life

Falling in love, there's nothing more pleasing,
It brings about such a warm and cosy feeling.
It can happen as quickly as a tropical downpour
Or nurtured over time leaving you lonely nevermore
With the former, I would advise you to proceed with caution
For one can all at once be consumed with a surge of emotion.
At which point the feeling sits on a fine line of fantasy and reality,
Confusing our minds with what could be a dangerous sense of urgency.
The heart will tell us to go with one's initial reaction
But for your sake, allow your head to sort out the attraction.
This is not to say that the power of kismet should be completely discounted,
More to the point, it is not wrong that this power should be confronted.
For perhaps those initial feelings may be more convincing if refined.
Far better than having to eventually admit that love was blind.

And to this, all I say having just experienced the latter,
Time has proven to be the winning factor.
For with him who I have come to believe is the true love of my life, it is clear,
As this feeling, felt from the start, but carefully nurtured for more than a year,
Has taught me a lesson I will now never forget
But for those to whom I gave my heart on a whim I refuse to regret.
As the accumulation of the disappointments and torment of my past,
I realise were put there to allow what I have now to forever last,
And to this end, may I plead to all whose resignation is that love is unbearably fleeting,
I would just like to say that everything in your past as painful as it might be seeming,
True love you will find, the love which is for you best suited
The love for which you have eagerly waited with breath that is baited.
The finite proof I now offer you is a man for whom my commitment will never wain.
My destiny, the love in my life that will forever remain.

Thirty-six

The danger in complacency

It's not what people say
More importantly how they say it.
With malice in their hearts
And reactions inappropriate.
Words that are not unfamiliar
Repeated day in and day out
What is this unwillingness and obstinance all about?
It can never bring us peace of mind
Nor a legacy for which we can be proud
It is a source of constant friction
A position that should never be allowed.
Let us continue the challenge
To each and every one of us.
To those who should know better and
To those who are completely clueless
I have become such a cynic at my age
So tiresome to read the same stories
My mind overworked, my heart in a rage
With those who have the power
To do the right things
Unfortunately, only focused advancing
Their own personal and selfish gains.
They prey on the weak and use that allegiance

To turn against those who suffer the same plight.
Who struggle day in and day out
Doing nothing more than trying to fight.
The injustice that inhibits a decent life,
These madmen using inhumanity like a knife.
What in the name of righteousness is that all about?
Cutting down the good in their own kind,
Putting the survival of our world into doubt.
It saddens me that these people are allowed
to propagate this indecency
But in the end, we are all guilty of fueling the fire with complacency.

Thirty-seven

Follow your own path with love

From the moment we're all brought into this world
The path we will take begins to unfurl.
It is at this crucial time we must be nurtured and loved
For only then can we inherit the desire to rise above
All the cruelty, negativity and judgement of a world gone mad.
The seemingly easy road taken by far too many, so naïve, so sad.
I am not one to believe that I stand alone in my struggle to find inner peace and self-worth,
For it is a journey we all face from birth
But it is that struggle which has caused all the chaos
By those who strive to separate themselves as better than the rest of us.
It is that mindset for whom I have come to take great pity,
For they will never understand the power they crave brings them such indignity.
Who are these people and why are they allowed to impact?
When it is difficult enough to keep our personal journey intact.

If the focus on our own positive growth is to be achieved,
Why do we crave the remedies of other whose sole purpose is to deceive?
The message should be crystal clear
And the outcome something we all must fear,
To that end, I would suggest that we never forget
Success is measured by having no regrets.
It is not measured through ill-gotten gain
Nor by criticising others for what we are not able to attain
Self-reliance and love in your heart is all we need in life
And as a part of all humanity, work to end those wanna-be demigods from causing terror and strife.
If love for ourselves and in turn for others is always our aim,
Peace, and a sense of belonging is what we all will gain.

Thirty-eight

Love now is but a roll of the dice

Here we go again, again, again
Will this heartache ever end?
Optimistically I play the game
Even though the results are always the same.
You'd think by now I would have learned
From all those times that I've been burned.
Bouncing from one attempt straight into another
Like moths flittering between lit lights with no bother.
I never thought I would be facing this heartache year in and year out
But having come this far into my journey there leaves very little doubt.
It has become more obvious that I won't escape this plight
For I no longer have the will to fight.
I'm truly tired of being on my own
For I was not born to go it alone.
In the end I suppose that I'm to blame
For I chose to move around too much in order to find fame.
Remember that old adage "The grass is always greener…"
One I wish now I would have headed instead I chose to be the big dreamer.

Had I known then what I know now
None of what has transpired would I allow.
It is at this point unmistakably clear
How I should have prioritised what I hold so dear.
But if finding love is at the top of your list
Stick to it and things won't go amiss.
Chose a locale and dive in for the long run
Make a life fulfilling and full of fun.
One that will attract as many possibilities as it can
Giving you the most opportunities to find the one and only man.
I wish I could heed my own advice
Unfortunately, my chances now are no greater than rolling the dice.

Thirty-nine

Hope is a double-edged sword

The road to happiness has been long and more often than not unattainable
With obstacles thrown in my path many of which seemingly insurmountable
I've never understood what seems to be an unfortunate fate
Always hoping beyond hope that a change will come before it's too late.
As the years have come and gone with no signs of a turnabout
The final outcome has cast upon my aspirations an ominous shadow of doubt
Sure, there have been many teasers to keep my dreams alive
But the sadness I feel always seems to survive.
Where do I go, how can I beat this terrible plight?
How much longer will I need to put up this flaying fight?
Hope by definition is a wonderful characteristic to possess
But given my experiences not proving helpful I must confess.

There is, though, an expression that seems more a propos
One that brings hope more into perspective as I've come to know
One that I now believe is a more fitting appraisal
Those famous or perhaps infamous words that "Hope Springs Eternal".

CPSIA information can be obtained
at www.ICGtesting.com
Printed in the USA
LVHW111421250719
625327LV00002B/240/P

9 781784 655372

CPSIA information can be obtained
at www.ICGtesting.com
Printed in the USA
LVHW111421250719
625327LV00002B/240/P

9 781784 655372